What Others Are Saying

"All the content is amazing. Totally useable and exciting to have in my toolkit for life. This stuff is so new and helpful and practical. I love it." CE

"The content helped me understand exactly what manifesting is and what I need to do to achieve my goals. It has allowed me to believe I can control my own destiny. So helpful." JO

"I love it. Truly. I wish I'd had this when I was 30 - would have been easier and more straightforward than stumbling onto this wisdom piece by piece over the decades through various therapies, self-help books, Al-Anon meetings, and life events that caused me to learn it the hard way." BF

"This has helped me access a deep sense of peacefulness inside of me and find some calm and ease. I now feel more positive and optimistic about my life I shall certainly keep coming back to the tools." AT

For more resources and insights, visit longandshort.co.uk.

For more resources and insights, visit <ins>longandshort.co.uk</ins>.

Practical Manifestation - The Magic Formula

For more resources and insights, visit longandshort.co.uk.

Practical Manifestation -
The Magic Formula
Transform Your Life -
Your Blueprint for Real Change

Lexie Bebbington and Carol Faculjak

LONG&
short

Publisher LONG & short

For more resources and insights, visit longandshort.co.uk.

Practical Manifestation - The Magic Formula
Transform Your Life - Your Blueprint for Real Change

Authors - Lexie Bebbington and Carol Faculjak
Publisher - LONG & short Publishing
Copyright ©2024 by LONG & short Publishing

LONG & short Publishing
longandshort.co.uk
ISBN - 9798334689497
First Edition
Printed in the United Kingdom

For more resources and insights, visit longandshort.co.uk.

Names - Bebbington, Lexie | Faculjak, Carol, authors.
Title - Practical Manifestation - The Magic Formula
Transform Your Life- Your Blueprint for Real
Change/Lexie Bebbington, Carol Faculjak.
Description - First Edition. | Includes bibliographical
references and index.
Identifiers - ISBN - 9798334689497 Subjects -
Manifestation (Spirituality) | Self actualisation
(Psychology) | Personal transformation.

Authors' Note

We wrote *Practical Manifestation - The Magic Formula*
to share the insights and strategies that have
genuinely transformed our lives and those of our
clients.

This book is a practical guide, filled with actionable
steps, to help you tap into your potential and
manifest what you truly want. We hope that this
book serves as a valuable tool in your life that you
can use over and over.

Here's to all of us finding our way forward with
our dreams and noticing all the glimmers along
the way.

Visit longandshort.co.uk for more information
on coaching, courses and resources.

Disclaimer

This book provides information on the subject matter but is not intended as legal, financial, or professional advice.

While we strive for accuracy, we make no guarantees. Please use this information as a guide and consult a professional for specific advice.

The authors and publisher are not responsible for any outcomes or damages resulting from its use.

Dedication

To all our incredible clients and course participants. This book is dedicated to each of you who has been along for the ride. Your courage, openness and commitment have been the heart and soul of our work.

Thank you for trusting us with your dreams and for inspiring us every step of the way.

Your dedication to living your best life has made this book possible, and we hope it serves as a testament to the power of manifestation and the magic that happens when we work together towards our goals.

For more resources and insights, visit longandshort.co.uk.

CONTENTS

For more resources and insights, visit longandshort.co.uk.

CONTENTS (continued)

For more resources and insights, visit longandshort.co.uk.

Introduction
The Power of Manifestation

Have you ever had that nagging feeling that you were destined for something more?

Do you ever notice others reaching new levels of success and wonder what makes the difference for them? Your life is going well but deep down you know there is more out there for you. What if the next step is just a small yet powerful change in how you see things?

If you've ever believed you are meant for more, you're not imagining it. This isn't just wishful thinking - it's a truth you may not have fully embraced yet.

For more resources and insights, visit <u>longandshort.co.uk</u>.

Right now, it's just hidden from view - this book is your practical guide to access that potential and finally create the life you love.

In *Practical Manifestation - The Magic Formula*, we don't just talk about what's possible - we show you how to make it happen, step-by-step.

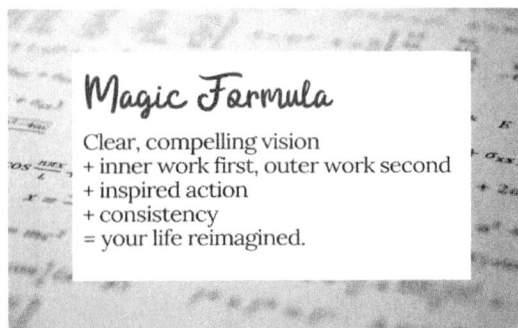

Magic Formula

Clear, compelling vision
+ inner work first, outer work second
+ inspired action
+ consistency
= your life reimagined.

Manifestation isn't just about dreaming big - it's like planting a garden where the seeds you sow represent your visions, dreams, and goals for the life you want. This systematic approach is your gardening plan, helping you nurture those seeds into flourishing realities.

What sets this book apart is its blend of practical, actionable steps with deep inner work, all designed to

For more resources and insights, visit <u>longandshort.co.uk</u>.

help you align with your true desires and take meaningful action.

Manifestation isn't just about thinking happy thoughts. Techniques like visualisation and positive affirmations can help rewire your brain to focus on achieving your goals by engaging its neuroplasticity. While it's not a magic trick, combining these practices with real action can genuinely help you move closer to what you want (Mind by Design, 2023; Positive Psychology, 2023)

Throughout this book, you'll discover helpful tools and practical steps to support you in moving towards a life you love. By following these steps, you'll have a clear path forward - and a calmer, more grounded mind to help you along the way.

This is your blueprint for real, sustainable transformation, and we are thrilled to be on this journey with you.

For more resources and insights, visit longandshort.co.uk.

"The best way
to predict the future
is to create it."

Peter Drucker

♡

For more resources and insights, visit longandshort.co.uk.

Chapter 1

Levels of Awareness in Manifestation

Understanding the different levels of awareness is the first step for mastering manifestation.

Imagine life as a river. Sometimes, we find ourselves swimming against the current, struggling and exhausted. Other times, we may be flowing smoothly with it, feeling aligned and at ease. And occasionally, we might not even be in the water, feeling disconnected and lost.

Knowing where you are in this river is essential.

For more resources and insights, visit <u>longandshort.co.uk</u>.

It allows you to adjust your approach, overcome obstacles, and move more effectively towards your goals.

But why do these levels of awareness matter so much? And how can they guide you towards living the life you truly want?

One of the most powerful aspects of our brain is its inherent capacity to reorganise and adapt, allowing us to develop new patterns of thinking and behaviour that align with our goals.

This phenomenon, known as neuroplasticity, is critical in shifting our awareness and mindset, and is essential for successful manifestation (MDPI's publication in *Brain Sciences* (2023).

For more resources and insights, visit <u>longandshort.co.uk</u>.

Victim Awareness

At this level, life feels like something that happens to you, rather than something you can influence. Picture yourself standing in the river, feeling the current drag you wherever it pleases. You feel powerless, stuck, and like a mere passenger in your own life.

Achiever Awareness

In this level, you understand that you have the power to take control and make a change. You choose to take decisive action and steer your life towards your desired path.

You decide to swim hard towards your destination. Here, you're actively trying to control the flow, pushing against the current with all your might.

You believe that if you just work hard enough, you can reach your goal. But this constant striving can also lead to burnout if you rely solely on force and effort.

For more resources and insights, visit longandshort.co.uk.

Flow Awareness

This is where the magic happens. In Flow Awareness, you move *with* the river, not against it.

Imagine yourself now, effortlessly gliding with the current, steering easily towards your goal. You're no longer struggling - you're in harmony with the natural flow of life. Opportunities seem to appear naturally, without force or struggle. This is the state where manifestation becomes effortless and intuitive.

Where Are You in the River?

Are you battling the current, feeling stuck and frustrated? Or are you flowing smoothly, embracing opportunities as they come?

If you find yourself thinking, "Nothing ever works out for me," you might be in Victim Awareness, where it's hard to see a way forward. Recognising this is the first empowering step. We won't leave you here - the rest of this book will guide you out of this mindset and into a place where the river flows easily.

For more resources and insights, visit longandshort.co.uk.

Maybe you're in Achiever Awareness, pushing hard but not seeing the results you want. The magic of manifestation truly reveals itself when you shift into Flow Awareness.

In Flow Awareness, you're not battling the current - you're moving with it, effortlessly seizing opportunities as they come. You might find yourself saying, "New opportunities are everywhere, and things are coming together so easily."

We begin here because understanding your position in the river - where your mindset and efforts are focused - determines how successful you'll be in manifesting the life you want.

In the chapters that follow, we'll provide simple tools to help you understand your position in this river and practical advice to shift from feeling stuck or fighting the current to a place where things flow more naturally.

For more resources and insights, visit longandshort.co.uk.

"The key to
manifestation is releasing
resistance and aligning
with the flow of the
universe, letting it work
through you."

Dr Wayne Dyer
♡

For more resources and insights, visit longandshort.co.uk.

Key Ideas

Levels of Awareness

- Recognising different levels of awareness is key to mastering manifestation – aligning thoughts, beliefs, and actions with what you truly want.
- Be aware of whether you're resisting, going with the flow, or standing still.

Victim Awareness

- Feeling powerless, as if life happens to you.
- Like standing in a river, feeling overwhelmed by the current.
- Change feels difficult, leaving you stuck or frustrated.

Achiever Awareness

- Realising you can shape your life through action. Like swimming hard against the current to reach your goal.
- Constant effort may lead to burn out without achieving the desired results.

Flow Awareness

- Moving with the flow of life instead of resisting it. Like swimming smoothly with the current towards your goal.
- Change becomes more effective and less exhausting.

Tools

Awareness Assessment Chart

Victim Awareness

1

Life is happening TO US, not something we can control. The current of the river pulls us wherever it wants.

Achiever Awareness

2

We take action at all costs, pushing hard against the current to reach the goal. Rely on force and effort.

Flow Awareness

3

Going with the river rather than forcing against it fighting it. Moving with the natural flow.

For more resources and insights, visit <u>longandshort.co.uk</u>.

For more resources and insights, visit <u>longandshort.co.uk</u>.

Chapter 2

Creating Your Clear, Compelling Vision

Manifestation always starts with a clear, compelling vision of what you want. Think of your vision as a detailed map guiding you to where you want to go, helping you understand each step along the way.

Attracting what we want starts with clarity and focus. The more specific and clear we are about our desires, the easier it becomes to align our thoughts, emotions and actions with those goals.

Tuning our mindset to the frequency of what we seek means focusing our thoughts and feelings on the outcome we want to achieve. It's about aligning our inner world - how we think and feel - with the goals we're aiming for, so that we naturally start to attract and notice opportunities that help us get there.

When our mindset matches what we desire, we're more likely to see and act on the things that bring us closer to our goals.

Scientific studies have shown that mental rehearsal using visualisation activates the same brain regions involved in actual performance, effectively "training" your brain for success by simulating the experience (Stanford Report, 2023).

When we focus on positive outcomes and truly believe that we deserve them, we naturally start drawing the right opportunities, people, and resources into our lives.

The power of attraction is the idea that positive or negative thoughts can bring positive or negative experiences into your life. Essentially, what you focus on in your mind can influence what happens in your reality (Psychology Today, 2023).

By holding a clear vision of what we want and staying open to receiving it, we create a magnetic pull that brings our desires closer to reality. Consistent belief and action reinforce this process, turning our aspirations into tangible results.

Make your vision vivid and specific. Use all your senses - what does it look like, sound like, and feel like?

Your level of awareness influences how clear and powerful your vision can be. If you're in Victim Awareness, feeling out of control, or in Achiever Awareness, constantly pushing yourself, it can be challenging to create a clear vision.

But when you focus on what you truly want and imagine it in detail, you shift from feeling scattered and exhausted to becoming focused and energised. This shift is key to reaching Flow Awareness, where everything feels easier.

For more resources and insights, visit longandshort.co.uk.

Take some time to visualise your ideal day.

Who are you with?

What are you doing?

How does it feel?

Writing down your vision can make it even more powerful. The more you can imagine and feel your vision, the stronger it becomes.

Consider the following to help you shape your vision.

What are you doing in your ideal life?

Where are you?

What can you see, hear, smell, touch, and taste?

Most importantly, how does it make you *feel*?

Even if visualising doesn't come naturally to you, just focusing on how reaching your goal will feel can be enough. The more you connect with that feeling, the more powerful the exercise becomes.

For more resources and insights, visit longandshort.co.uk.

To effectively manifest your dreams, it's essential to engage all your senses when visualising your goals.

By vividly imagining what you see, hear, smell, taste, and feel, you create a more compelling and tangible picture in your mind, making it easier to turn that vision into reality.

The more sensory details you include, the stronger your connection to your goal becomes, guiding your actions with clarity and intention.

For example, if your goal is to open a successful yoga studio, imagine the soft sound of calming music playing in the background, the scent of lavender and eucalyptus filling the air, and the feel of the smooth yoga mat beneath your feet as you guide a class through a series of peaceful poses.

For more resources and insights, visit longandshort.co.uk.

Imagine you're designing your dream garden. Envision the vibrant colours of the flowers, each petal catching the sunlight just right. Smell the fresh, crisp scent of the morning dew on the grass as you walk barefoot. Hear the sound of a gentle breeze rustling through the leaves, and the peaceful chirping of birds that have made your garden their home.

By using your senses to create these vivid images, you can make your vision more real and attainable, setting the stage for turning your dreams into reality.

We'll explore how to bring this vision to life in more detail in the coming chapters.

Life Pie Chart

When envisioning your ideal life, it's easy to focus on specific goals, but true fulfilment comes from considering all aspects of your life. This is where the Life Pie Chart comes in. It encourages you to look at key areas like career, relationships, health, personal growth, and leisure. Dream big and create a vision for each area of your life.

For more resources and insights, visit longandshort.co.uk.

At the end of this chapter, you'll find a Life Pie Chart and questions to help you explore these areas. There are no right or wrong answers - just be honest about where you are now and what you want. Dive deep into each area and discover what you truly desire.

This isn't just a one-time exercise - it's your blueprint you can use whenever you want to create something new in your life.

Visualisation strengthens our goals by activating specific areas of our brains. When we vividly imagine achieving a goal, our brains process it as if it's real, reinforcing our commitment and making it much more likely we'll achieve our goals.

To really solidify your clear, compelling vision, try spending a few minutes each day visualising your ideal life. This simple practice helps you feel more connected to your goals, making it much easier to take steps towards them.

For more resources and insights, visit longandshort.co.uk.

Vision Boards

If you've heard of vision boards and wondered what they're about, they're a great tool for solidifying your clear, compelling vision. A vision board is like a magical collage of your dreams and goals - a creative way to clarify what you want in life and set your intentions in motion.

It is a visual representation of your goals and dreams, usually made up of images, words, and quotes that symbolise what you want. Think of it as a personal mood board that reflects your desires and motivates you to act towards them. The beauty of a vision board is that it's unique to you - no two are ever the same.

Creating a vision board helps you get really specific about what you want. Sometimes our desires are vague but putting them down on paper forces us to be clear. Do you want a new job? A healthier lifestyle? More travel? A vision board helps you pinpoint exactly what you're aiming for.

Seeing your vision board every day keeps your goals top of mind. Put it somewhere you'll see it often. The idea is that looking at your vision board feels good and serves as a reminder of what you're working towards.

Vision boards keep you focused and motivated, even on days when you're feeling off track. They should be packed with positive images and affirmations that boost your mood and mindset.

When you're surrounded by visual reminders of your goals, you're more likely to stay positive and motivated - key ingredients for manifesting your dreams.

At the end of this chapter, you'll find a fun, step-by-step guide on how to create your own vision board.

For more resources and insights, visit <u>longandshort.co.uk</u>.

"The future belongs to those who believe in the beauty of their dreams."

Eleanor Roosevelt

♡

Key Ideas

Start with a Clear, Compelling Vision

- The more specific and clear you are about your desires, the easier it becomes to align your thoughts, emotions, and actions with those goals.

- Engage all your senses to create detailed and vivid mental images that bring your vision to life.

Visualisation Practice

- Spend a few minutes each day visualising your ideal life. Focus on daily activities, your surroundings, and emotions.

Life Pie Chart

- Create an ideal scenario for all the aspects of your life - career, relationships, health, personal growth, and leisure.

Vision Boards

- Create a visual representation of your goals and dreams. Use images, words, and quotes that symbolise what you want and make sure it elicits the feelings you want to experience. Display it where you'll see it daily for motivation.

For more resources and insights, visit longandshort.co.uk.

Tools

YOUR LIFE PIE

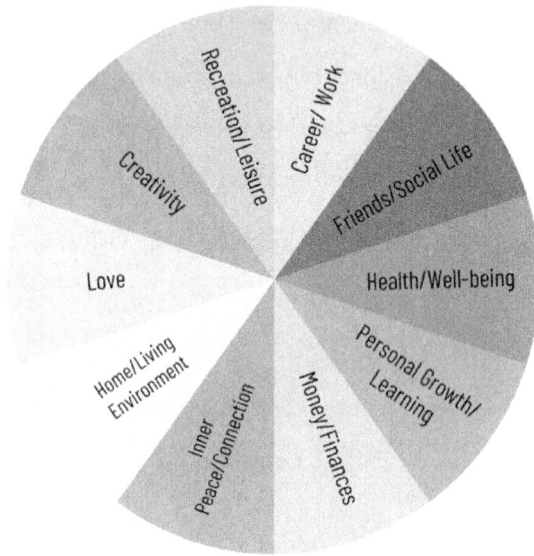

The Life Pie Chart helps us to review all the key areas of our lives, like pieces of a puzzle that fit together to create a balanced and fulfilling picture.

Use the questions on the next pages to explore your ideal scenarios in each area and set clear, specific goals. This exercise guides you to envision and create a life you love.

For more resources and insights, visit longandshort.co.uk.

Be as specific as you can about your goals in each area.

Career/Work

- What does my dream job look like? ·
- What kind of work excites me?
- How do I want to feel?

Friends/Social Life

- What does an ideal relationship with my friends look like?
- How would I describe my perfect social life?
- Who do I want in my life?

Health/Wellbeing

- What does being in good health mean to me?
- How do I want to take care of myself physically and mentally?
- What habits make me feel vibrant and healthy?

Personal Growth/Learning

- What new things would I love to learn?
- How do I see myself growing and developing?

For more resources and insights, visit longandshort.co.uk.

Money/Finances

- What does financial security look like for me? ·
- How would I feel with all my financial goals met?
- What are my biggest financial dreams?

Inner Peace and Connection

- What does it mean for me to feel truly fulfilled on a spiritual level?
- How can I strengthen my connection to myself, the world around me, and something greater?
- What practices or beliefs bring me a sense of calm and peace?

Recreation/Leisure

- What activities bring me joy and relaxation?
- How would I like to spend my free time?
- What new adventures or hobbies would I like to explore?

For more resources and insights, visit longandshort.co.uk.

Home/Living Environment

- What does my ideal home look and feel like?
- How do my surroundings inspire me and bring me joy?
- What changes would help my living space feel good to me?

Love

- Imagine feeling deeply loved and appreciated. What does that look and feel like?
- How do I express love to others, whether friends, family, or a partner?

Creativity

- What activities ignite my creativity the most?
- How do I express my creativity in my everyday life?
- What does the perfect environment look like for nurturing my creativity?

For more resources and insights, visit longandshort.co.uk.

How to Make Your Vision Board

Vision boards help us focus on our goals by visualising them and keeps us on track. What we focus on tends to grow and become more important in our lives. By directing our attention to positive goals or feelings, we can attract more of those positive experiences into our world.

Choose Your Materials

Use a large piece of paper, poster board, or corkboard. Digital versions also work, but there tends to be something extra special about crafting your board by hand.

Set the Mood

Creating a calming environment using candles, meditation, or uplifting music can offer something special to the vision board building experience.

For more resources and insights, visit longandshort.co.uk.

Pick Your Focus

Decide on the area of life you most want to work on. You can make one main board or several smaller ones, but a central board often works best. You can always create more vision boards later. In fact, we encourage it!

Gather Inspiring Images

Choose images and words that represent your goals as if you've already achieved them. Use whatever works for you, including magazines, online images, or personal photos.

Make It Personal

Add personal symbols, photos, or quotes that inspire you. Use colours and fonts that light you up and resonate with your vision.

Place It Where You'll See It

Keep your vision board where you'll see it daily - maybe inside your wardrobe door, where you'll notice it every day as you get dressed. Another idea is to give it pride of place on your living room wall.

Whatever works best for you is perfect.

For more resources and insights, visit longandshort.co.uk.

Share Your Vision

Talk about your vision board with people you trust, if that feels right for you. Sharing can help make it feel real, build confidence and create accountability.

If that doesn't feel comfortable, another option is to journal about it instead. In this way, you are sharing your vision board more deeply with yourself.

Enjoy creating your vision board, and let it guide you towards achieving your dreams.

For more resources and insights, visit longandshort.co.uk.

Chapter 3

Doing the Inner Work

Now that you have a clear, compelling vision in place, the next step is the inner work.

"Inner work" simply means calming your mind and tuning into your intuition to help achieve your dreams.

Inner work can shift our level of awareness, helping us move from Victim or Achiever Awareness to Flow Awareness. This chapter will provide techniques and tools designed to calm the mind and tune your intuition. Research shows that maintaining a peaceful mind through mindfulness and meditation helps reduce

For more resources and insights, visit longandshort.co.uk.

negative thoughts, making it easier to hear your inner voice and make better decisions (Harvard Gazette, 2023). This state of calm and focus supports more effective decision-making and better management of challenges (Knowledge at Wharton, 2023).

Grounding ourselves mentally and emotionally is important preparation for effective action. A simple phrase to help us remember the most powerful order of things is "inner work first, outer work second."

Imagine for a moment that your mind is like a still pond. When the pond is calm, you can see reflections clearly and make decisions with minimal effort.

However, when the pond is disturbed, the reflections become muddled and clarity fades – so calming the mind whenever possible makes a significant difference to the quality of our thinking and the actions we decide to take.

Feeling good now is a powerful manifestation concept. It's about deliberately choosing to feel good, no matter what. This doesn't mean ignoring or suppressing tough

For more resources and insights, visit longandshort.co.uk.

emotions. It's important to acknowledge and experience all our feelings.

However, once we have felt our feelings, we actually have more power than we realise to choose how we want to feel.

By consciously shifting our attention towards more uplifting emotions, we can harness that positive energy to attract more good things into our lives. And the great news is that the more we choose to do this, the easier it gets.

When we find ways to feel those positive feelings, it naturally puts us in what we call *the Manifestation Slipstream* - the fast lane to achieving what we want.

We all know those times when it can feel very much like we're stuck in the slow lane, bogged down by low moods and feelings of "yuck." Everything feels sluggish and stagnant when we are in this place.

However, when we realise we can *choose* to change our state of mind, something almost magical happens. It's

For more resources and insights, visit <u>longandshort.co.uk</u>.

like we begin to automatically merge into the fast lane, where everything flows more smoothly. Try it out and see for yourself -you'll be amazed what shows up!

Take the time to notice all the synchronicities that begin to appear. Celebrate them. Acknowledge them.

"What we appreciate, appreciates." This means that when we show gratitude for the good things in our lives, we attract even more positive experiences.

The techniques below are all about helping you feel more grounded, calm, and ready to attract the good stuff into your life whenever you need it.

Mindfulness

Mindfulness is a simple way to feel calmer and more grounded. It's about being fully present in the moment without getting lost in thoughts or judgments. Instead of letting your mind run wild, focus on what's happening right now.

Notice your thoughts and feelings without getting wrapped up in them - just let them drift by like clouds in the sky. At first, it might feel a bit strange, but with practice, it gets easier.

Mindfulness isn't just about finding peace in the moment - it has the power to rewire your brain Studies have found that practicing mindfulness can actually thicken areas of the brain related to memory, emotions, and self-awareness, which helps explain why people often feel better mentally and emotionally after meditating (Harvard Gazette, 2011)

These brain changes back up the idea that mindfulness meditation can have real, positive effects on your overall mental health (Neuroscience News, 2023).

For more resources and insights, visit longandshort.co.uk.

Regular mindfulness practices can lead to enhanced focus, resilience, and reduced stress by altering the neural structures involved in attention and emotional regulation.

This means that the more you engage in mindfulness, the more you strengthen your brain's ability to stay calm and focused, even in challenging situations.

Breathing
Breathing exercises are a quick and effective way to bring calm and focus into your day. They help improve your mood by calming your nervous system and reducing stress.

Start by finding a quiet spot, sitting comfortably, and closing your eyes. Take a slow, deep breath in through your nose, letting your belly expand like you're filling a balloon. Hold the breath for a moment, then exhale slowly through your mouth. Repeat this a few times, and you'll feel the stress start to melt away.

Another great technique is Box Breathing. Breathe in for four seconds, hold for four, exhale for four, and hold

For more resources and insights, visit longandshort.co.uk.

again for four. Repeat this cycle a few times, and you'll begin to feel more centered.

You can also try the 4-7-8 Breathing method. Breathe in quietly through your nose for four seconds, hold for seven, and then exhale completely through your mouth for eight. Do this four times to ease any anxiety and promote relaxation.

If you want to explore more, you can search online for more resources. Look for "Breathwork for Stress Relief" or "Deep Breathing Techniques."

Meditation
Meditation is another fantastic way to calm your mind and reduce stress. It's as simple as focusing on one thing at a time, like your breath or a soothing sound.

Think of it as a mini-holiday for your brain, helping you feel more peaceful and clear-headed. Regular meditation can also help change your brain, boosting your mood and focus while calming the parts that handle stress.

For more resources and insights, visit longandshort.co.uk.

There are many ways to meditate, from guided sessions to just sitting quietly and focusing on your breath. The key is consistency - even short, regular meditation sessions can make a big difference in how you feel.

Affirmations

Affirmations are positive statements that you repeat to yourself to reinforce new, empowering beliefs. They work by helping your brain build new pathways that support positive thinking and behavior. Studies show that this practice can boost your self-esteem and reduce stress by activating the brain's reward centers (Psychology Today, 2021). The trick is to make them feel real and achievable.

Start with small, believable statements like "I'm getting better at my job every day" or "I'm making healthier choices."

As you continue to practice these affirmations and tie them to your daily actions, they start to rewire your thinking, making positive changes feel not only possible but also a natural part of your life.

This consistent practice helps your mindset align with your goals, making the process of achieving them feel more effortless and within reach.

Tackling Limiting Beliefs

Limiting beliefs are those negative thoughts that hold you back, like "I'm not good enough" or "I'll never succeed." These beliefs often come from past experiences or things you've been told.

To break free from them, start by questioning if they're really true. Look for evidence in your life that disproves them - you'll likely find plenty.

For instance, if you think "I'm terrible at public speaking," remember times when you've spoken well, maybe even to a small group of friends. Reflect on these successes, and you'll start to replace those limiting beliefs with more empowering thoughts that actually help you grow.

Journaling

Journaling is a great way to get in touch with your thoughts and feelings. Writing things down helps you

For more resources and insights, visit longandshort.co.uk.

process emotions, gain insights and track your growth. Research shows that journaling can reduce stress, improve your mood and enhance self-reflection.

By regularly recording your experiences, you create a space to understand yourself better and see things from a new perspective. Over time, journaling can become a meaningful habit that adds richness and depth to your life.

Taking Care of Yourself
Don't forget about simple self-care - it's crucial for staying balanced and grounded. Simple things like reading a good book, going for a relaxing walk, or spending time with people you like or your pet can do wonders for your well-being.

These little acts of kindness towards yourself help keep your mind calm and make it easier to stay on track, even when life gets tough.

By weaving these tools - mindfulness, breathing, meditation, affirmations, challenging limiting beliefs, journaling, and self-care - into your life, you can take

For more resources and insights, visit longandshort.co.uk.

charge of how you feel in any moment and move you into the Manifestation Slipstream more easily.

You'll start to feel more anchored, confident, and ready to manifest the good things you want. At the end of this chapter, you'll find some tips and tricks to help you dive deeper into these practices and find the ones that work best for you.

"If you don't go within.
you go without."

Neale Donald Walsch

♡

Key Ideas

Inner Work Basics

- Inner work means calming your mind and tuning into your intuition. It helps shift awareness from Victim or Achiever to Flow Awareness.

- Feeling positive feelings naturally puts you in the Manifestation Slip Stream - the fast lane to achieving what you want.

- A peaceful mind makes it easier to hear your inner voice and attract what you want. It supports thoughtful decisions and makes handling challenges easier.

Helpful Techniques for Inner Work

- Mindfulness
- Breathing
- Meditation
- Affirmations
- Tackling limiting beliefs
- Journaling
- Taking care of yourself

For more resources and insights, visit longandshort.co.uk.

Tools

Affirmations

Positive affirmations are short, powerful statements that help you feel good now, overcome negative patterns, and reinforce a belief in yourself.

Why Affirmations Matter

- Rewire thought patterns - repeated affirmations can change the neural pathways in your brain.
- Counteract negativity - they help fight back against self-doubt and fear.
- Fuel growth - affirmations remind you of your capability and potential.

How to Use Affirmations

- Choose affirmations that resonate - pick statements that feel meaningful and true to you.
- Repeat daily - say them out loud, write them down, or reflect on them.
- Visualise - imagine the affirmations coming to life. Feel the emotions as if they are already true.

For more resources and insights, visit longandshort.co.uk.

- Be consistent - the more you use them, the easier it is to rewire your brain and integrate these positive beliefs into your life.

Tips for Integrating Affirmations

- Sticky notes - write affirmations on sticky notes and place them in places you look regularly.
- Set reminders - use your phone to set daily reminders for your affirmations.
- Journal - dedicate a section of your journal to writing affirmations.
- Voice recordings - record yourself saying your affirmations and listen to them frequently.

For more resources and insights, visit <u>longandshort.co.uk</u>.

Affirmations to Try

Gratitude and Appreciation

- I wake up each morning with a grateful heart and an open mind.
- I say thank you for all the wonderful things in my life.
- I appreciate all that I have.

Self-Belief and Confidence

- I believe in myself.
- ·I am increasingly confident in my ability to create the life I want.
- ·When I focus on feeling good now, I make better choices that lead to more of what I want.

Creating Positivity

- I am acting on my own inspiration and insights, and I know I can trust my intuition.
- My dreams are manifesting before my eyes.
- I attract wonderful experiences, meaningful connections and what is meant for me.

For more resources and insights, visit longandshort.co.uk.

Contribution and Love

- I am worthy of love, abundance, success, happiness and fulfilment.
- I contribute goodness to the world, and I am well-compensated for what I offer.

Abundance and Prosperity

- I am receiving abundance in expected and unexpected ways.
- I always have enough to fulfil my needs.
- Every day, in every way, my life becomes richer, better and more abundant.

For more resources and insights, visit longandshort.co.uk.

Your Journal

Your journal is more than just a bunch of pages. It's your secret hideout through life's wild adventures, a VIP ticket to the movie of your life where you can rewrite the story of your destiny.

Life can be a roller coaster with loads of surprises, some good and some not so good, but this journal is your go-to friend when you need a break.

Why Journal?
As you attract opportunities, you'll realise that your outer world reflects your inner world. Your thoughts are the sturdy table, and your positive affirmations are the legs that hold it up. A single piece of evidence may leave your thoughts a bit wobbly, but with lots of evidence, your thoughts become super strong.

By keeping a journal of all the positive things happening in your life, you're training your brain to notice more good things, and it's telling your brain, "Hey, this stuff works! Good things happen to me, and it feels

For more resources and insights, visit longandshort.co.uk.

amazing!" With more and more positive experiences, you'll start believing that it's the real deal.

Your journal is like a treasure trove of all the magical moments in your life. It captures both unexpected, jaw-dropping moments and tiny specks of happiness that affirm your path and remind you of your dreams and desires. These moments are gems that can shape your reality over time.

Tips and Tricks for Using Your Journal

Daily Entries

- Write about your day, focusing on the positive experiences and moments of gratitude.
- Include even the smallest wins and joys. They all add up!

Positive Affirmations

- Start your day by writing a few affirmations.
- Reinforce these throughout your journal entries.

For more resources and insights, visit longandshort.co.uk.

Visualisation

- Describe your dreams and goals as if they've already happened.
- Paint a vivid picture with words, detailing how you feel in those moments.
- Use these to help you *feel good now*.

Gratitude Lists

- Regularly jot down things you're grateful for. This shifts your focus to the good in your life, reinforcing positive thinking.

Mindset Shifts

- Note any changes in your mindset or perspective.
- Recognise how these shifts help you attract more of what you want.

Creative Expression

- Use drawings or doodles to inspire or express creativity

For more resources and insights, visit longandshort.co.uk.

Chapter 4

Feeling Your Feelings

Getting to know and truly experience our emotions is like unlocking a hidden strength that can help us achieve our goals. The big challenge is that many of us fear our own feelings and worry that we won't be able to handle them.

Because of this fear, we often shove down emotions like anger, sadness, fear, guilt, anxiety, shame and loneliness.

For more resources and insights, visit longandshort.co.uk.

These feelings can seem overwhelming or too risky to confront, so we distract ourselves with things like overeating, excessive drinking, scrolling, shopping, smoking, gambling, or even obsessively going to the gym.

But here's the thing. When we allow ourselves to fully feel our feelings - even the uncomfortable ones -we actually help them to dissolve and dissipate. Once we understand this, it makes moving forward so much easier, clearing the way for growth and change.

The truth, which many of us were never taught, is that **all our feelings really want is to be felt**. We think they need to be analysed, dissected, or endlessly chewed over. They really really don't. They simply need to be experienced. That's it.

It's such a simple concept that it's easy to miss its importance. But once we really get this, we can approach our emotions in a completely different way - and when we do, our lives begin to change for the better in more ways than we can imagine.

For more resources and insights, visit <u>longandshort.co.uk</u>.

Feeling your feelings is good for you because it helps your brain process emotions and prevents them from building up and causing stress or anxiety. Research shows that when you allow yourself to experience emotions, you can actually improve your mental health and resilience (Harvard Health, 2020; American Psychological Association, 2019).

Emotions are like weather patterns moving across the sky. Just as storms eventually give way to clear skies, our feelings ebb and flow. When strong emotions arise, they can feel like a brewing storm - intense and overwhelming - but remember, storms are temporary. They may be powerful for a time, but they are always passing on through.

The key is to allow yourself to just be *with* these emotions - to be patient, and weather the storm. This means experiencing what you're feeling without judging it - without labelling it bad or wrong or "too much".

For more resources and insights, visit longandshort.co.uk.

This acceptance helps us become the observer of our feelings, knowing they will eventually clear and that they cannot actually hurt us.

When a tough emotion shows up, gently let yourself feel it. Stay out of your mind and bring your attention into your body where the feeling is. Notice the sensations. It is safe to let yourself feel them.

When we allow our feelings just to be and exist rather than pushing them away, they lose a lot of their negative power.

It is helpful to remember that feeling all kinds of emotions is a natural part of being human. Encourage acceptance by thinking, "I allow myself to feel these feelings without judging them or myself." And most importantly, remind yourself, "I can breathe into the feeling and relax. It is safe for me to feel this feeling."

As we mentioned in Chapter 3, breathing consciously is very helpful with all inner work, and feeling our feelings is no exception. Breathing isn't just about survival – it doubles up as a great tool for managing intense emotions and calming the body's stress response. It helps us move from emotional turbulence to a balanced state, guiding us towards that gentle state of Flow Awareness. Focus on deep, slow breaths when uncomfortable feelings arise.

This sends a signal to our brain to relax, reducing our stress levels and helping us to feel more grounded and balanced. Imagine your breath as a gentle breeze, calming a storm within. Each deep breath acts as a soothing wave, settling the turbulence.

Feeling our feelings fully is also a powerful way to create space for fresh, new thinking to show up. It opens us up to our intuition. Think of dissolving uncomfortable feelings as like cleaning out old, cluttered drawers. By clearing out the junk, we make room for new, exciting opportunities to flow in.

If you are willing to master the art of feeling your feelings fully, your entire life will change. You'll soon start to notice a greater sense of emotional freedom and resilience begin to bubble up. This freedom comes

For more resources and insights, visit longandshort.co.uk.

from knowing that, no matter what feelings arise, **you can handle them**.

This is a big deal.

At first, fully feeling your emotions might take some courage, but it's worth it.

Being okay with whatever comes up is a powerful step towards achieving your dreams.

For more resources and insights, visit longandshort.co.uk.

"Feelings are just visitors,
let them come and go."

Maoji

♡

Key Ideas

Importance of Emotions

- All feelings just want to be felt.

- Feeling emotions is key to achieving goals and suppressing your emotions can lead to stress.

- Be willing to experience the full range of feelings It is reassuring to realise you can feel them fully without having to act on them.

- Feeling feelings fully helps clear the way for growth and change.

- Emotions are like weather patterns, temporary and changing.

- Sit with emotions without judgment, knowing they will pass.

Breathing Exercises

- Deep, slow breaths help manage intense emotions.

- Calm the body's stress response and aids in maintaining Flow Awareness.

For more resources and insights, visit <u>longandshort.co.uk</u>.

Emotional Freedom

- Embracing feelings leads to emotional freedom and resilience.

- This builds confidence and reduces fear of change.

Treat Feelings Kindly

- Be patient and kind to yourself.

- Emotional resilience paves the way to achieving your dreams.

For more resources and insights, visit <u>longandshort.co.uk</u>.

Tools

Ideas to Help Feel Your Feelings

- Chat with a supportive friend, write in your journal, dive into a creative project, or go for a walk or a run.
- Get fresh air. Take 5 slow deep breaths - Inhale calm, exhale stress.
- Indulge in a small luxury and really savour it.
- Treat yourself to your favourite meal.
- Take a warm, soothing bubble bath.
- Capture at least five joyful moments with your camera today.
- Listen to some music you love.
- Write a note of appreciation to your body for all it does.
- Practice a boundary and politely decline something you don't want to do.
- List 10 things you love about yourself (and maybe even decorate it with hearts.)
- Wear something that makes you feel good.
- Spend five minutes in quiet, electronic-free bliss.
- Shift from "I can't" to "what if" and open your mind to potential opportunities.

For more resources and insights, visit longandshort.co.uk.

Chapter 5

Breaking up with Complaining

There's no doubt that complaining can feel satisfying in the moment - whether it's about the weather, the traffic, or that annoying colleague at work - but it's actually doing us so much more harm than good.

When we complain, we are stuck in Victim Awareness. If we focus on solutions and gratitude instead, we get to lift ourselves out of that mindset and start making positive changes.

Think about how draining it is to be around someone who's always complaining. It not only increases our stress levels, but it can also drag down our mood and our relationships suffer as a result.

Complaining is contagious too - when we complain, other people often can't resist jumping right in there with us, fanning the flames. This can make small problems seem huge and we end up focusing on what isn't going well in our lives.

So, here's your challenge - break up with complaining.

We know it sounds tough, but it really is one of the best things you can do for yourself - especially if you're committed to achieving your dreams.

When we stop complaining, we naturally start focusing on solutions, which has the added benefits of lowering our stress levels and helping us feel calmer and more balanced.

A positive attitude also has a ripple effect, making our interactions with other people more enjoyable, improving our relationships and helping us handle our challenges more effectively too.

Breaking the complaining habit doesn't mean ignoring problems or pretending everything is perfect. Life will *always* have its ups and downs - we'll still have rows with the people in our lives and tricky projects at work and traffic to contend with.

It's about shifting our focus from what is beyond our control to what we actually *can* do. This subtle shift can make a surprising difference when it comes to reaching goals.

Here's a simple yet powerful idea to help you shift your mindset and bring more positivity into your day - wear a piece of jewellery, like a bracelet or ring as a gentle reminder to stay positive.

Whenever you catch yourself about to complain, touch the jewellery and take a moment to think of something that feels just a little better, more productive, or helpful instead.

For more resources and insights, visit longandshort.co.uk.

If you want to take it up a notch, try wearing a rubber band on your wrist. Whenever you find yourself slipping into negativity, give it a gentle snap. This small action can create a brief pause, giving you the chance to redirect your thoughts and think something more positive.

It's a simple habit, but over time, it can make a big difference in how you feel and how you approach life.

Keeping a gratitude journal is another great way to stay more positive. Each day, write down three things you're thankful for, no matter how small - like a good meal or a sunny day or fresh, clean sheets on the bed. Reflecting on these positives can help balance out any complaints and keep us focused on the good stuff.

Surround yourself with people who lift you up. Fun, supportive friends and family can make it so much easier to stay focused on your goals and boost your own feel-good factor. Their good vibes are contagious and make everything look that bit brighter.

Breaking up with complaining also helps us stop seeing ourselves as victims and start seeing the truth of ourselves as people capable of creating our own reality.

Instead of saying, "I can't find time to exercise," we might think, "I can make time to exercise because it's important to me." This simple shift can make such a difference.

Be prepared for the possibility that breaking the complaining habit might take a little time. It's okay to slip up now and then, especially if it's been a long-standing habit.

When that happens, cut yourself a bit of slack and then deliberately refocus your thoughts on something positive.

Over time, you'll develop a new habit where it feels more natural to focus on what you like rather than what you don't.

For more resources and insights, visit longandshort.co.uk.

To stay on track, we recommend setting small goals for yourself. Start by aiming to go a whole morning without complaining, then work up to a full day, then two days and then a week.

Notice how this new positive habit is affecting your life and helping you *feel good now* and get even closer to living a life you love.

"The more you complain
about your problems,
the more problems you
will have to complain
about."

Zig Ziglar

♡

For more resources and insights, visit longandshort.co.uk.

Key Ideas

Impact of Complaining

- Keeps us in Victim Awareness.
- Negatively impacts mood and motivation.

Giving up Complaining

- Reduces stress and promotes good feelings.
- Enhances emotional well-being.
- Encourages you to focus on what you want, rather than what you don't.
- Moves focus from helplessness to empowerment.

Practical Tips

- Use jewellery or a rubber band as a reminder to stay positive.
- Keep a gratitude journal to focus on things that light you up.
- Surround yourself with positive and supportive people.
- See yourself as the creator of your reality.
- Focus on what you can control and improve.

For more resources and insights, visit longandshort.co.uk.

- Be patient with yourself and celebrate small successes.

- Gradually build up the habit of being complaint-free.

For more resources and insights, visit <u>longandshort.co.uk</u>.

Tools

Changing Complaints into a Positive Mindset

Changing how we think about problems can turn challenges into opportunities for growth. Here are some common complaints, each with an alternative way of looking at them to help us learn and grow.

Complaint - "I always fail at this."
Reframe - "Each time I try, I learn more about what doesn't work, bringing me closer to finding what does."

Complaint - "I can't do this - it's too hard."
Reframe - "This challenge is an opportunity for me to grow and improve my skills."

Complaint - "I hate making mistakes."
Reframe - "Mistakes are actually learning experiences that help me improve."

Complaint - "I'm not good at this."
Reframe - "I'm not good at this *yet*, but with practice, I can improve."

Complaint - "I'll never be as good as them."
Reframe - "I can learn from others and strive to reach my own potential."

For more resources and insights, visit <u>longandshort.co.uk</u>.

Complaint - "I don't understand this."
Reframe - "I don't understand this *yet*, but I can ask questions and seek help to learn more."

Complaint - "This isn't fair."
Reframe - "Life has its ups and downs, but I can control how I respond and make the best out of any situation."

Complaint - "I'm terrible at this."
Reframe – "Everyone starts somewhere. I can get better with effort and persistence."

Complaint - "This is taking too long."
Reframe - "Progress takes time, and every step forward is a step towards my goal."

Complaint - "I always get so overwhelmed."
Reframe - "I can break this down into smaller, manageable tasks."

For more resources and insights, visit <u>longandshort.co.uk</u>.

For more resources and insights, visit <u>longandshort.co.uk</u>.

Chapter 6

The Magic of Gratitude

Gratitude can really change your life. It's like a superpower that makes you happier, strengthens your relationships and even helps you reach your dreams.

Gratitude might be a buzzword these days, but it's actually a time-tested practice that's been embraced by people across the globe for centuries. Long before modern life became so hectic, wise individuals from different cultures knew that gratitude wasn't just a nice idea - it was essential for living a fulfilling life.

For more resources and insights, visit longandshort.co.uk.

From ancient philosophers to spiritual traditions, the act of appreciating what we have has always been seen as a cornerstone of happiness. In a world that often nudges us to focus on what's missing, gratitude helps us reconnect with the richness of what's already in front of us, offering a refreshing perspective that can lead to a more joyful, contented life.

Gratitude plays a big role in manifestation by helping you focus on the positive aspects of your life, which can attract more good things your way.

When you regularly practice gratitude, it shifts your mindset to abundance rather than lack, making it easier to believe that your desires can become reality (Psychology Today, 2021; Greater Good Science Center, 2020).

Gratitude is about noticing and appreciating the good things in our life, no matter how small. Whether it's a sunny day, laughing with friends, or even a tough lesson learned, taking a moment to say "thank you" helps shift our focus from what we're missing to what we already have. And that small change can make a big difference.

Practicing gratitude is really just another way of saying *feel good now*. When we focus on what we're grateful for, we naturally start to feel better. This good feeling is like a magnet for more positive experiences.

If we're always complaining or focusing on what's wrong, we attract more negativity. But when we're thankful, we naturally invite more good things into our lives to be thankful for.

For example, if you're looking for a new job, instead of focusing on what you don't like about your current situation, start being grateful for the skills you've gained, the experiences you've had, and the opportunities you're hoping for. It might not be easy at first, but this shift in focus can open new possibilities.

Gratitude changes our brains, helping us become more positive and resilient. It makes it easier to see the good in every situation, which boosts our overall well-being.

Plus, as a bonus, it strengthens our relationships. When we show appreciation for the people in our lives, it deepens our connections and builds trust, like planting seeds of kindness that grow into strong bonds.

Taking time to reflect on what we're thankful for, especially before bed, can also help us sleep better. It's a simple way to calm our minds and drift off more easily.

Gratitude also makes us mentally stronger, helping us bounce back from tough times with a positive attitude.

Sharing our gratitude with others is another powerful way to spread good vibes. Thank the people who support and inspire you, whether it's through words or simple gestures. You might be surprised at how much a little appreciation can brighten someone's day and create a ripple effect of kindness.

Glimmers

Glimmers are tiny moments that bring joy and calm, like finding a rainbow after a storm or discovering a forgotten fiver in your pocket. These small joys lift us up and help us feel more connected to the present moment.

For more resources and insights, visit longandshort.co.uk.

Focusing on glimmers helps shift our attention away from stress and negativity. By looking for and appreciating these positive moments, we're training our brains to see more of the good in life.

Over time, this practice can make us happier and more relaxed. It's like giving our brains a little dose of sunshine every day.

The great news is that glimmers are everywhere - a beautiful sunset, a warm hug, or that first sip of your morning coffee. Start looking for these moments to turn the ordinary into the extraordinary. Try setting a simple goal each day, like "Today, I'm going to notice all the little joys around me." You'll find it's easier than you think!

To keep track of these moments, you might want to incorporate them into a Gratitude Journal practice or start a fun Glimmer Journal - a place where you can write down the things that make you smile. You can even take pictures of them to create a visual diary. Sharing these snapshots online can be a fun way to inspire others.

For more resources and insights, visit longandshort.co.uk.

Be open to surprises, too. The best glimmers often come from unexpected places. When we welcome these moments with an open heart, they can bring us the greatest joy.

Once you start noticing glimmers in your daily life, you'll see some amazing changes. Your mood will improve, and you'll become more resilient. These small joys help you relax and recover more quickly from life's challenges too.

As we train our minds to focus on the good, we naturally start to feel happier and more fulfilled. This growing sense of gratitude helps us see the world through a fresh, new lens - and life just feels better.

Gratitude and glimmers are like perfect partners in helping us live our best lives.

For more resources and insights, visit <u>longandshort.co.uk</u>.

"The more you are in a
state of gratitude, the
more you will attract
things to be grateful for."

Rhonda Byrne

♡

Key Ideas

The Power of Gratitude

- Gratitude makes you happier, strengthens your relationships, and helps you reach your goals.
- It shifts your focus from what's missing to what you already have.
- It moves you from feeling stuck or Victim to a satisfying state of Flow Awareness.

Benefits of Gratitude

- Gratitude rewires your brain to be more positive and resilient.
- It deepens connections with others, building trust and stronger bonds.
- Practicing gratitude boosts your health and reduces stress.
- Make it a habit to be thankful every day, even for the small stuff.
- Keep a journal to note down things you're grateful for.

For more resources and insights, visit longandshort.co.uk.

Glimmers

- Glimmers are tiny moments that bring joy and calm, lifting your moods.

- Focusing on glimmers helps you stay positive.

- They activate relaxation and counteract stress.

For more resources and insights, visit <u>longandshort.co.uk</u>.

Tools

A Little Guide to Glimmer Hunting

Set an Intention

Start your day with the intention to notice as many glimmer as you can. Actively LOOK for them. Setting this intention can prime your mind to be on the lookout for positive moments.

Be Present

Start by being intentional and try to notice things fully present in the moment. Pay attention to your surroundings and your feelings.

Use Your Senses

Engage all your senses. Notice the small details like the warmth of the sun, the smell of coffee, or the sound of the wind in the trees.

Slow Down

Take your time. Don't rush through your day. Slowing down even a little is enough to notice the tiny moments of joy.

Be on the Lookout

Focus on positive interactions and events, no matter how small. A smile from a stranger, a kind word, or a break in the clouds can be a glimmer.

Use the Glimmer Tracker (under Tools)

Write down the glimmers you notice. Keeping a record helps you remember and appreciate these moments more deeply.

Share with Others

Talk about your glimmers with friends or family. Sharing positive experiences can enhance the joy they bring.

Be Patient

Don't get discouraged if you don't notice glimmers right away. With practice, it will become easier to spot them.

For more resources and insights, visit <u>longandshort.co.uk</u>.

Glimmer Spotting & Tracker

Tracking glimmers helps you become more aware of positive moments, boosting your mood and resilience. This practice encourages mindfulness and gratitude, leading to a happier and healthier mindset.

Date	Glimmer	How it Made Me Feel	Notes

For more resources and insights, visit longandshort.co.uk.

Chapter 7

Unlocking Your Brain's Innate Focus Power

This chapter explains how you can harness your brain's built-in radar to enhance your manifestation practice and bring your desires into reality.

The Reticular Activating System (RAS) is like a personal assistant in your brain, constantly filtering the flood of information around you to focus on what's most relevant.

This network of neurons in the brainstem plays a critical role in determining what grabs your attention, helping you process sensory information.

For more resources and insights, visit longandshort.co.uk.

Research highlights the critical role the RAS plays in filtering information and maintaining focus, making it a key player in the process of manifestation (Healthline, 2023; Simply Psychology, 2022).

By tuning into what matters most, the RAS helps you stay alert and concentrated on your goals. When you understand how to leverage your RAS, you can shift the way you interact with the world, making it a powerful ally in your manifestation journey.

For instance, have you ever thought about buying a specific car and suddenly noticed that model everywhere? That's your RAS at work, highlighting what's important to you at the moment and filtering out the rest.

You can intentionally guide your RAS to help you achieve your goals. Imagine you're aiming for a promotion at work. You've set clear intentions, identified the skills you need, and created a vision board filled with images of success and leadership. Every morning, you affirm, "I am a valuable asset to my team and ready for a leadership role." With your

For more resources and insights, visit longandshort.co.uk.

RAS tuned into this vision, you start noticing opportunities that align with your goal - like hearing about a new project or finding a relevant training program. Your RAS is steering you towards actions that bring you closer to that promotion.

The same principle applies if your goal is to become fitter and healthier. By defining what fitness looks like for you and surrounding yourself with positive affirmations and visuals, your RAS will help you notice healthier options and opportunities, making it easier to stick to your fitness routine and achieve your goals.

The key to effectively training your RAS lies in repetition and clarity. The more you focus on your goals through visualisation and positive affirmations, the more your RAS reinforces that focus, keeping you on track.

Think of your RAS as a radar, constantly scanning for opportunities that align with your desires and helping you take steps towards them.

For more resources and insights, visit longandshort.co.uk.

One crucial aspect of this process is positive self-talk. Your RAS thrives on affirmations like "Every step I take brings me closer to my goals" or "I am learning and growing every day." If you catch yourself slipping into negative thoughts, gently replace them with thoughts that feel better. Over time, this practice strengthens your RAS's ability to guide you towards success.

In essence, your RAS is a powerful tool that, when harnessed correctly, can help you focus on what's important, recognise opportunities and take actions that support your dreams. It's like having a built-in guide that keeps you aligned with your goals and helps you filter out distractions.

By understanding and working with your RAS, you can make your manifestation practice more effective and transformation.

For more resources and insights, visit longandshort.co.uk.

"Your focus determines your reality."

George Lucas

♡

Key Ideas

- The Reticular Activating System (RAS) is your brain's filter on what gets your attention.

- You can use the RAS to focus on what matters to you.

- The RAS highlights things you've been thinking about.

- Setting intentions helps the RAS spot helpful opportunities.

- Repetition and visualisation strengthen the RAS's focus.

- Positive self-talk helps the RAS support goals.

- The RAS filters out distractions, keeping you focused on what's important.

- The RAS acts as a radar, scanning for info to help you.

For more resources and insights, visit <u>longandshort.co.uk</u>.

Tools

Turbocharge Your RAS

Daily Goals Reminder

- Write down your top 3 goals on a small piece of card.
- Review them every day, morning and evening.
- Imagine how it will feel when you achieve them.

Focus Objects

- Select a small object and carry it with you. (e.g. a small stone, or a special coin).
- Each time you touch it, remind yourself of your main goal. Savour how it feels.

Reflection

- End each day by answering these reflective questions -
  - o What went well today?
  - o What did I learn?
  - o What can I do tomorrow to move closer to my goals?

For more resources and insights, visit longandshort.co.uk.

Consume Positive Media

- Choose to consume media that aligns with your goals and makes you feel good.

- Unfollow, block, or delete accounts, pages, or content that trigger you.

- By removing negative influences, you create a more positive and encouraging environment that supports your well-being and personal growth.

Appreciation Alarm

- Set an alarm to go off at the same time each day. When it rings, pause and envision achieving your goal.

- Appreciate the wonderful feeling of your future accomplishment.

For more resources and insights, visit longandshort.co.uk.

Chapter 8

The Power of Feelings

Manifesting really works best when we focus on the positive emotions that come with achieving our goals, rather than stressing about the steps (the how) to get there.

The "how" often gets in the way of our dreams by causing us to overanalyse and doubt ourselves before we even start.

For instance, if you dream of starting your own business, you might get so caught up in worrying about funding, finding customers or managing

For more resources and insights, visit <u>longandshort.co.uk</u>.

logistics that you become overwhelmed and paralysed, never even taking the first step.

Instead of focusing on the excitement and passion that sparked the dream in the first place, we let the fear of not knowing every detail block our progress, keeping us stuck where we are.

Instead of getting bogged down by the details of *how* it will happen, when we shift your attention to how it will *feel* once our goals are realised, the emotional alignment naturally guides the "how" to fall into place.

Imagine the joy, satisfaction, or sense of accomplishment you might feel when you have what you most want. This connects you emotionally with your future success, which is a powerful motivator.

When we feel these positive emotions, we create a strong mental and emotional link to our goals, making them feel much more real and attainable. For instance, if your goal is to give a talk on stage, imagine the thrill and satisfaction you'll feel when you hear the audience applaud. Feel it fully. Hear the clapping. See their faces. Let it sink in and feel real.

The more real you can make your dreams in your imagination, the more powerful the manifestation process will be for you.

Another example could be if your goal is to run a marathon. Picture yourself crossing the finish line, the crowd cheering, your strong legs carrying you forward, and a medal being placed around your neck. Feel the sense of accomplishment and pride in your hard work and dedication.

By feeling these emotions deeply and vividly, we strengthen our motivation and make the process of achieving our goals feel more attainable and real.

Scientists have found that regularly practicing visualisation can significantly boost motivation and confidence by helping the brain prepare for success by creating vivid mental images of achieving goals.

For more resources and insights, visit <u>longandshort.co.uk</u>.

The process of visualising success not only primes the brain for the actual experience, making it easier to take the necessary steps toward those goals, but it also strengthens the neural pathways associated with positive outcomes. This reinforcement builds the motivation and confidence needed to pursue goals effectively (Wu Tsai Neurosciences Institute, 2024, Fastlane Freedom, 2024).

When you visualise your goals, your brain activates and strengthens the same neural pathways used when performing actual tasks, essentially "training" your brain for real-life actions. Visualisation is a powerful technique that also helps reduce stress and anxiety, making it easier to stay focused and motivated as you work towards your goals.

Research has shown that by regularly practicing visualisation, individuals can shift their attention away from negative thinking patterns, reducing feelings of stress and anxiety. It helps create calmness in both the mind and body.

For more resources and insights, visit longandshort.co.uk.

Visualisation exercises, such as imagining peaceful scenes, help in releasing muscle tension and lowering stress hormone levels, contributing to overall emotional well-being (Verywell Mind 2023, Aura Health 2023).

That's why many athletes, entrepreneurs, and other successful people make visualisation a key part of their training routines.

When we choose to focus more on the destination, we want to reach than the route needed to get there, the "how" tends to take care of itself. And by focusing on the good feelings, you'll find you naturally attract opportunities and actions that align with these feelings.

This weirdly simple approach can do wonders for the manifestation process.

It's like setting our internal SAT NAV towards our desired feelings, and the route to get there becomes clearer as we go.

For more resources and insights, visit longandshort.co.uk.

It's Already Yours

Acting like you've already achieved your goals is another game-changer when it comes to manifesting what you want.

When you carry yourself as if your dreams are already reality, you're basically telling your mind, "It's already mine!" This mindset boosts your confidence and shuts down any doubts that might creep in.

Plus, when you act like it's already yours, you naturally start making choices and taking steps that align with that vision. It's like you're paving the way for your dreams to actually come true because, in your mind, they already have.

Have you noticed we don't need to know the entire route to get to a destination using our SAT NAV – we just need to know the next turning to take? Remembering this can make the whole process so much more enjoyable and is great for taking the pressure off too.

For more resources and insights, visit longandshort.co.uk.

Consider creating a list of the positive feelings you aim to experience and let this list guide your daily actions. By actively connecting with these feelings, it paves the way to make decisions and take actions that propel you towards your goals

For instance, if your goal is to boost your confidence, you might start by speaking up more in meetings, even if it's just to ask a question or offer a brief comment.

Each time we do this, we step slightly out of our comfort zones, which gradually builds confidence. You may start to notice new opportunities for advancement or collaboration that weren't even apparent before.

Give it a try, and you might be surprised by how quickly your confidence grows and how many new doors begin to open.

Remember, focusing on how it will feel when you achieve your goals creates a powerful driving force.

For more resources and insights, visit longandshort.co.uk.

It helps you overcome challenges and stay committed, making the journey to success much more enjoyable.

When you encounter obstacles (which are inevitable), remind yourself of the incredible feeling you'll have when you cross that finish line

For more resources and insights, visit longandshort.co.uk.

"I am where I am
because I believe
in possibilities."

Whoopi Goldberg

♡

Key Ideas

Focus on Feelings

- Concentrate on the positive emotions of achieving goals, not the steps to get there.
- Imagine the joy and satisfaction of reaching your goals.
- Make these feelings vivid and real.

Let the "How" Unfold

- Focus on desired feelings, and the steps will become clear.
- Like using a SAT NAV, you only need to know the next turn.

It's Already Yours

- Acting as if your goals are already achieved helps solidify your belief in them.
- This makes it easier to attract and manifest what you desire.

Daily Actions/Feelings

- Create a list of positive feelings you aim to experience.

- Let this guide your actions and decisions.

- Act as if it is ALREADY YOURS!

For more resources and insights, visit longandshort.co.uk.

Tools

Cultivate Positive Feelings

While all feelings just want to be felt, you can choose to focus on positive ones to enhance your well-being. Decide what you want to experience more of and start each day with an intention to focus on it.

"Today I Want to Feel …"

Joyful	Creative
Confident	Bold
Excited	Thrilled
Calm	Spontaneous
Grateful	Invigorated
Loved	Cheerful
Content	Flexible
Hopeful	Compassionate
Inspired	Curious
Serene	Fulfilled
Enthusiastic	Peaceful
Proud	Happy
Flexible	Empowered
Optimistic	Relaxed
Trusting	Bold
Appreciated	Thrilled
Playful	Spontaneous
Resilient	Invigorated
Secure	Cheerful
Patient	Compassionate
Adventurous	Curious

Chapter 9

Inspired Action-
Where the Rubber Hits the Road

Taking inspired action is what bridges the gap between dreaming and doing. It's the moment you shift from just planning to actually making your vision a reality.

Think of inspired action as rowing a boat down a river. Without rowing, your boat drifts aimlessly, carried wherever the current takes it. But when you do the inner work first and then pick up the oars and row, you find yourself moving closer and closer to where you want to go.

For more resources and insights, visit longandshort.co.uk.

Inspired action is different from ordinary effort - it comes from being deeply aligned with your vision and intuition. Unlike forced action, which feels like struggling against the current, inspired action feels as though the river is working with you.

More often than not you will still need to do some rowing - but it will feel easier, more natural, and less like you're fighting the flow. You won't need to push yourself so hard, you'll simply follow what feels intuitively right.

Focus on your clear, compelling vision of what you truly want to achieve, and then identify the actions that align with that vision. Trust the hunches and intuitive impulses that show up and follow them whenever you can. Even though you will still need to row, you'll find that you're no longer forcing your way forward but moving in unison with the river's natural flow.

When you have clarity about your vision and are doing the inner work, you'll start to feel a gentle pull towards certain actions. These actions feel effortless and aligned, as if the river itself is guiding you.

For more resources and insights, visit <u>longandshort.co.uk</u>.

Trust these impulses and follow them, knowing they are leading you towards your desired outcome.

To identify your inspired actions, take some time to brainstorm or journal about what steps feel exciting or quietly "right." This is the power of the inner work.

For example, if you're planning to start your own graphic design studio, your vision might include a creative workspace full of activity, satisfied clients, and the joy of turning your passion into a thriving business. You've set clear intentions, created a vision board with inspiring designs and affirmations like "I am a thriving graphic designer."

Inspired action is the bridge between this vision and reality. Instead of getting overwhelmed by all the steps, start with small, intuitive actions that excite and guide you. Maybe you begin by taking an advanced design course to refine your skills. As you improve, your confidence grows.

At a local art fair, you meet an established designer whose work you admire.

For more resources and insights, visit longandshort.co.uk.

The conversation flows easily, and they offer valuable business tips and even suggest a collaboration. This is a sign that you're on the right path.

You also start creating custom designs for friends and local businesses, getting feedback to refine your style. This process is fulfilling and fuels your passion. One day, you find the perfect space for your studio in an artsy part of town. You feel a surge of excitement and decide to secure the space, feeling that everything is falling into place.

Each of these steps is an example of inspired action. They're not forced or stressful - they flow naturally from your vision and feel energising. By following these inspired actions, you move closer to making your dream studio a reality. This is the power of aligning your actions with your inner guidance and vision.

Remember, inspired action doesn't always mean big leaps. Small, consistent steps also create significant progress over time. Each small action is like adding a pebble to a path, steadily building a clear route towards your goal.

For more resources and insights, visit <u>longandshort.co.uk</u>.

And if you're not sure what to do next, just do something - *anything*. Sometimes, just taking one step can open the floodgates to new, inspired ideas.

Be patient and stay open to adjustments. The course you set initially may need to shift as you go. Navigating a river often means steering around obstacles. This flexibility keeps you on course while adapting to new circumstances and opportunities. Sometimes, the most challenging parts of the journey offer the greatest growth.

When taking inspired action, stay open to feedback and new information. Being adaptable ensures you keep moving forward, even when the path ahead isn't clear. This approach keeps you connected to your vision and helps you make the most of every opportunity. In other words, see everything as an opportunity - how great is that?

Surrounding yourself with a supportive community that encourages you can be helpful. You might want to share your goals and progress with people who uplift and

For more resources and insights, visit <u>longandshort.co.uk</u>.

motivate you. Their encouragement and insights can guide you and keep you accountable to your vision.

A supportive network can be a source of inspiration and strength, helping you stay committed and celebrating your achievements along the way.

For more resources and insights, visit longandshort.co.uk.

"The journey
of a thousand miles
begins with one step."

Lao Tzu

♡

For more resources and insights, visit <u>longandshort.co.uk</u>.

Key Ideas

- Inspired action turns dreams into reality - it's the step between imagining and achieving.

- Purposeful actions move you forward - like rowing a boat, each move brings you closer to your goals.

- Trust intuitive nudges - follow what feels right to guide you effortlessly.

- Small, exciting steps build momentum – these actions keep you moving towards your dreams.

- Adapt plans as needed - adjusting your path helps you stay on track and seize new opportunities.

- Consistent efforts matter - regular small actions lead to significant progress.

- Be flexible - stay open to changes and new information to keep moving forward.

For more resources and insights, visit longandshort.co.uk.

Tools

Break it Down into Mini Goals

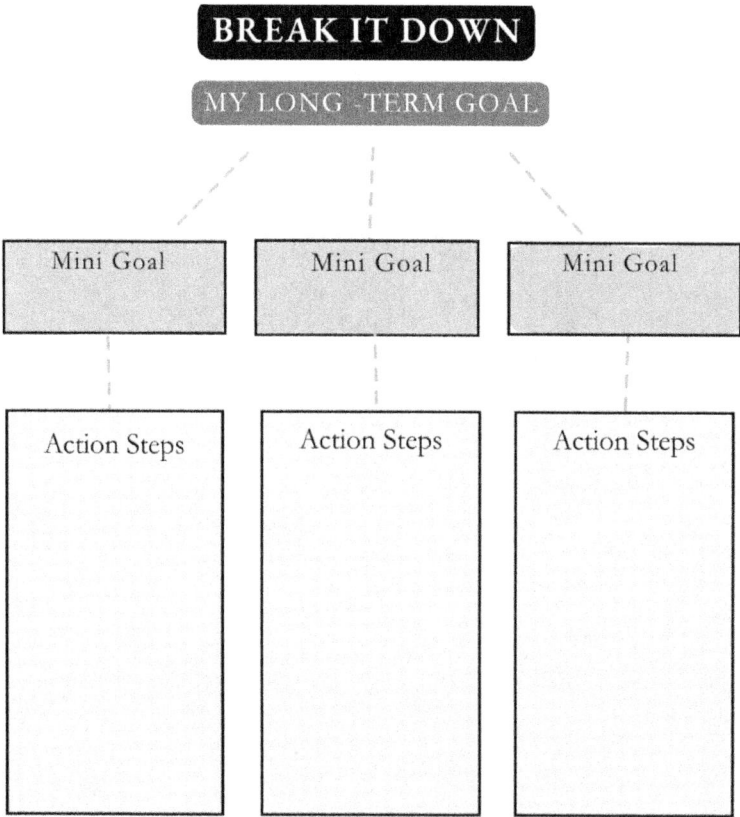

BREAK IT DOWN

MY LONG-TERM GOAL

Mini Goal	Mini Goal	Mini Goal

Action Steps	Action Steps	Action Steps

For more resources and insights, visit <u>longandshort.co.uk</u>.

Chapter 10

Maintaining Consistency

Consistency is the steady rhythm that keeps us moving towards our goals. It acts as the heartbeat of our manifestation journey, providing a reliable pulse that fuels our progress.

Just as a musician will practice regularly to improve, maintaining consistency in our actions strengthens our paths towards success.

Consistency acts as the steady rhythm that drives our manifestation journey forward.

For more resources and insights, visit longandshort.co.uk.

Consistency is important for your brain because it strengthens the connections between neurons, making it easier to build and stick to habits. When you repeat an action regularly, your brain gets better at it, helping you do it more automatically over time (Neuroscience News, 2022; Psychology Today, 2020).

This process reinforces the behaviours that match our goals, making it easier to maintain those positive habits. Over time, these actions become more automatic, almost like our brain is setting them on autopilot, which deeply ingrains them into our daily routines.

It is no secret that consistency means sticking to your plan and keeping up your efforts, even if your motivation dips. Now, with this new understanding, you know the formula to get yourself back on track whenever you feel derailed. By committing to steady, small actions and trusting in the process, you now know you can regain your momentum and continue progressing toward your goals.

Think of a plant that needs watering every day. The steady care ensures it will grow strong and healthy, reaching towards the light. Similarly, consistent effort nurtures our goals, allowing them to flourish.

Regularly checking on our progress and celebrating small wins reinforces our commitment. Each accomplishment, no matter how tiny, represents a milestone on our journey.

Viewing these micro achievements as important steps towards our larger goals makes it easier to stay motivated and on track.

Although consistency is important, it doesn't mean being rigid. Just as a river flows around obstacles and changes course, adapting our approach is often needed to make progress.

Embracing the natural flow of life and allowing for adjustments while remaining committed to our overall direction is a life-long learning curve.

For more resources and insights, visit longandshort.co.uk.

Accountability becomes our best friend when we are trying to be consistent. Sharing our goals with a friend, group, workshop, or coach introduces a comfortable layer of external support and encouragement.

Setbacks and obstacles really are natural parts of the journey. Choosing to view each challenge as an opportunity to grow stronger, wiser, and more resilient builds inner strength which keeps us going. This resilience helps us move forward, no matter what obstacles arise.

The fundamental driving force for any goal is your WHY.
Why are you doing it?
What's important about it?
How will you feel when it's real?

Finding your why is about uncovering the deeper purpose that fuels your goals and dreams. It's the spark that ignites your passion and keeps you moving forward, even if things get tough.

For example, if you're working towards a promotion, your why might be the desire to provide a better life for your family or to achieve personal growth and recognition in your field.

If you're aiming to adopt a healthier lifestyle, your why could be to have more energy to play with your kids or to feel confident and vibrant in your own skin.

Perhaps you dream of traveling the world – your why might be the excitement of experiencing new cultures and the adventures that come with it.

By identifying these core motivations, we create a powerful anchor that keeps us grounded and focused on our journeys.

This makes the pursuit of our goals more meaningful and fulfilling and ultimately plays an important role in bringing them to life.

For more resources and insights, visit longandshort.co.uk.

"Success is the sum
of small efforts, repeated
day in and day out."

Robert Collier

♡

For more resources and insights, visit longandshort.co.uk.

Key Ideas

Importance of Consistency

- Keeps you steadily moving towards your goals.
- Fuels progress with a reliable, steady rhythm.

Accountability

- Sharing goals with others offers support and encouragement.
- Helps maintain focus and motivation.

Celebrate Small Wins

- Regularly check progress and celebrate each achievement.
- Small wins are milestones towards bigger goals.

Flexibility

- Be adaptable like a river navigating obstacles.
- Adjust your approach while staying true to your overall direction.

For more resources and insights, visit <u>longandshort.co.uk</u>.

Finding Your Why

- Discover the deeper purpose behind your goals.

- Understand the motivation and passion to drive yourself forward.

Tools

Daily Habits Tracker

Tracking your daily habits is another simple way to see your progress and stay motivated. By noting down activities like glimmer spotting, practicing a positive mindset, or completing tasks from your inspired action list, you can celebrate small wins each day. This makes your journey towards your vision exciting and rewarding.

Plus, it helps you stay focused and see how even the smallest actions can lead to big results. Use the daily habits tracker to remind your Reticular Activating System (RAS) that you are actively working towards your goals.

By consistently recording your progress, you signal to your brain that these actions are important. This keeps your goals at the forefront of your mind, helping you notice more opportunities and stay motivated on your journey.

For more resources and insights, visit longandshort.co.uk.

Habit Tracker

Date: _____   Week: _____

Habits	Sun	Mon	Tue	Wed	Thu	Fri	Sat
1 _____	○	○	○	○	○	○	○
2 _____	○	○	○	○	○	○	○
3 _____	○	○	○	○	○	○	○
4 _____	○	○	○	○	○	○	○
5 _____	○	○	○	○	○	○	○
6 _____	○	○	○	○	○	○	○
7 _____	○	○	○	○	○	○	○
8 _____	○	○	○	○	○	○	○
9 _____	○	○	○	○	○	○	○
10 _____	○	○	○	○	○	○	○
11 _____	○	○	○	○	○	○	○
12 _____	○	○	○	○	○	○	○
13 _____	○	○	○	○	○	○	○
14 _____	○	○	○	○	○	○	○
15 _____	○	○	○	○	○	○	○
16 _____	○	○	○	○	○	○	○
17 _____	○	○	○	○	○	○	○
18 _____	○	○	○	○	○	○	○
19 _____	○	○	○	○	○	○	○

For more resources and insights, visit longandshort.co.uk.

Chapter 11

Embracing Your Reimagined Life

Congratulations on finishing *Practical Manifestation - The Magic Formula!*

Getting to this point shows your commitment to making real changes in your life, and that's something worth acknowledging.

Now that you've explored these concepts, you'll notice a shift in your perspective. You're truly imagining what it feels like to achieve your goals. You are taking the inspired, concrete steps to make them a reality.

You have the ability to shape your mindset from the inside out, and that's powerful.

With the tools and insights you've gained, you can now choose thoughts that lift you up, focus on *feeling good now,* and take actions that align with what you truly want.

As you continue to apply these tools in your life, remember that the power of manifestation is not just an abstract concept - it's rooted in our biology and psychology.

The practices you've learned are supported by scientific research, which shows that the brain can be rewired for success through consistent, focused effort, as these practices strengthen neural pathways and enhance cognitive functions, making it easier to achieve and maintain goals (Tackle Tough Things, 2023, MentalHealthDaily, 2023).

By sticking to these practices, you can make lasting changes that help you reach your full potential and live the life you've always dreamed of.

Here's your magic formula again.

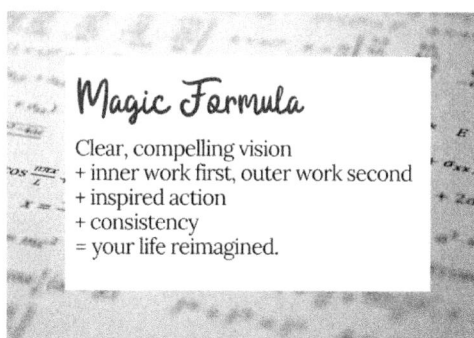

Magic Formula

Clear, compelling vision
+ inner work first, outer work second
+ inspired action
+ consistency
= your life reimagined.

You've learned how to identify where you stand, map out a clear vision, and use practical tools to keep your mind calm and focused.

You also understand the value of taking action that feels right and staying consistent.

As you move forward, think about where you are right now. Are you resisting, going with the flow, or adjusting as needed?

Knowing this helps you decide your next steps and stay focused on what matters most.

For more resources and insights, visit longandshort.co.uk.

Manifesting is like weaving a tapestry from your thoughts, actions, and emotions. Each choice adds to the design of your life. Keep adding new threads that make your life richer and more colourful, more YOU.

This process is ongoing. Your goals and vision might shift along the way and that's perfectly fine.

Embrace those changes and stay open to what's possible. Your life is your creation, constantly evolving. Celebrate what you're building and recognise how far you've come.

Every step in your life has contributed to where you are now, showing your growth and resilience. Your life reflects your choices and the effort you've put in. Stay focused on what feels right for you, and trust that you have everything you need to create the life you want.

The future is yours to shape, so go out there and make it happen.

After all, it's already yours!

For more resources and insights, visit longandshort.co.uk.

"Whatever the mind can conceive and believe, it can achieve."

Napoleon Hill

♡

Key Ideas

- Acknowledge your achievement - reaching the end of this book is a great start to creating the life you want.

- Embrace your power - you are actively shaping your life and learning that you have control over your inner world.

- Apply the magic formula of clear compelling vision, inner work, inspired action, and consistency to manifest a life you love.

- Recognise your progress - identify where you are in your journey and adjust as needed.

- Celebrate the journey - view manifestation as a tapestry where each experience and action adds depth and richness to your life.

- Stay open to change - be adaptable and embrace new possibilities, knowing that your vision and goals can evolve along the way.

For more resources and insights, visit <u>longandshort.co.uk</u>.

Manifesting Means

Dreams coming to life
Me thriving
You thriving
All of us thriving
Allowing life to surprise us
Love that lasts
Unexpected bouts of creativity
Strong, healthy, independent kids
Serendipitous moments
Whispers of adventure
Heartfelt connections
Cosy nooks
Having plenty of money
Deep sighs of contentment
Epic journeys
Brilliant conversations
Effortless elegance
Talking about how great we are doing
Loving our pets as best friends
Feeling good in our skin
Joyful parenting
Feeling truly loved
Sunkissed days
Gratitude felt in our core
Generous hearts
Delicious moments
Being ourselves everywhere we go
Getting everything we want
Wanting everything we have

For more resources and insights, visit longandshort.co.uk.

For more resources and insights, visit <u>longandshort.co.uk</u>.

INDEX OF TOOLS

For more resources and insights, visit longandshort.co.uk.

For more resources and insights, visit <u>longandshort.co.uk</u>.

REFERENCES

Chapter 1: Levels of Awareness in Manifestation

- MDPI's publication in *Brain Sciences* (2023): Discusses neuroplasticity and its role in shifting awareness and mindset, which is essential for successful manifestation.

Chapter 2: Creating Your Clear, Compelling Vision

- Stanford Report (2023): Research on how mental rehearsal using visualisation activates the same brain regions involved in actual performance, effectively "training" your brain for success.
- Psychology Today (2023): Explains the power of attraction, showing that what you focus on in your mind can influence what happens in your reality.

Chapter 3: Doing the Inner Work

- Harvard Gazette (2023): Discusses how mindfulness and meditation help reduce negative thoughts, making it easier to hear your inner voice and make better decisions.
- Knowledge at Wharton (2023): Provides insights on how a calm and focused mind supports better decision-making and management of challenges.

For more resources and insights, visit <u>longandshort.co.uk</u>.

REFERENCES (continued)

- Harvard Gazette (2011): Explores how mindfulness can thicken areas of the brain related to memory, emotions, and self-awareness, positively affecting mental health.
- Neuroscience News (2023): Confirms the positive brain changes resulting from regular mindfulness practices, including enhanced focus and reduced stress.

Chapter 4: Feeling Your Feelings

- Harvard Health (2020): Discusses how feeling your emotions helps the brain process them, preventing stress and anxiety.
- American Psychological Association (2019): Provides evidence that experiencing emotions improves mental health and resilience.

Chapter 6: The Magic of Gratitude

- Psychology Today (2021): Explains how gratitude shifts your mindset to abundance, aiding in manifestation.
- Greater Good Science Center (2020): Supports the idea that practising gratitude can attract more good things into your life by changing your mindset.

For more resources and insights, visit longandshort.co.uk.

REFERENCES (continued)

Chapter 7: Unlocking Your Brain's Innate Focus Power

- Healthline (2023): Discusses the role of the Reticular Activating System (RAS) in filtering information and maintaining focus, key for manifestation.
- Simply Psychology (2022): Explains how the RAS helps keep you alert and focused on your goals.

Chapter 8: The Power of Feelings

- Wu Tsai Neurosciences Institute (2024): Highlights how regular visualisation boosts motivation and confidence by training the brain for success.
- Fastlane Freedom (2024): Reinforces the idea that visualising success strengthens neural pathways associated with positive outcomes.
- Verywell Mind (2023): Shows how visualisation reduces stress and anxiety, contributing to emotional well-being.
- Aura Health (2023): Discusses the benefits of visualisation exercises in lowering stress hormone levels and creating calmness in the mind and body.

For more resources and insights, visit longandshort.co.uk.

REFERENCES (continued)

Chapter 10: Maintaining Consistency

- Neuroscience News (2022): Provides insights on how consistency strengthens neural connections, making it easier to build and stick to habits.

- Psychology Today (2020): Explains how regular actions reinforce behaviours that align with your goals, making them more automatic over time.

Chapter 11: Embracing Your Reimagined Life

- Tackle Tough Things (2023): Discusses how consistent, focused effort rewires the brain for success by strengthening neural pathways.

- MentalHealthDaily (2023): Explains how these practices enhance cognitive functions, making it easier to achieve and maintain goals

For more resources and insights, visit longandshort.co.uk.

About the Authors

Lexie Bebbington and Carol Faculjak first crossed paths at a CoActive Training Institute coaching class in London in 2004. Since then, they've not only transformed hundreds of lives but have also been each other's support throughout their coaching journeys.

Known for their passion for personal growth and a heartwarming blend of expertise and empathy, they've guided countless clients towards lives that are happier, more focused, and deeply fulfilling.

In this book, they draw on their extensive experience in manifestation and coaching to create a supportive and inspiring guide aimed at helping you achieve your dreams.

Besides running their own individual coaching practices, Lexie and Carol also team up to conduct workshops, courses, and collaborate on special projects - including this book! They bring their collective wisdom and infectious enthusiasm to everything they do, aiming to make a positive impact in every life they touch.

Visit longandshort.co.uk to find out more about courses, coaching and free resources.

NOTES

For more resources and insights, visit <u>longandshort.co.uk</u>.

NOTES

For more resources and insights, visit <u>longandshort.co.uk</u>.

NOTES

Printed in Great Britain
by Amazon

47509586R00089